Meade Heights Elementary School

Presented to the Library

1995 by 902d MI Group

in memory of SGM Robert Wheeler

A ROOKIE BIOGRAPHY

MARGARET WISE BROWN

Author of Goodnight Moon

By Carol Greene

Teachers, parents, and others interested in knowing more about
Margaret Wise Brown may wish to consult *Margaret Wise Brown:
Awakened by the Moon* by Leonard S. Marcus (Beacon Press, 1992).

 CHILDRENS PRESS®
CHICAGO

Margaret Wise Brown (1910-1952)

Library of Congress Cataloging-in-Publication Data

Greene, Carol.
   Margaret Wise Brown—author of Goodnight moon / by Carol Greene.
     p. cm. — (A Rookie biography)
   Includes index.
   Summary: A simple biography of the author who, during her short life,
wrote over 100 books for young children.
   ISBN 0-516-04254-8
   1. Brown, Margaret Wise. 1910-1952—Biography—Juvenile literature.
2. Authors, American—20th century—Biography—Juvenile literature.
[1. Brown, Margaret Wise. 1910-1952. 2. Authors, American.] I. Title.
II. Series: Greene, Carol. Rookie biography.
PS3503.R82184Z67
813'.52—dc20
[B]
                                     92-34471
                                       CIP
                                       AC

Margaret Wise Brown
was a real person.
She lived from 1910 to 1952.
Margaret wrote many
books for children.
One was *Goodnight Moon*.
This is her story.

TABLE OF CONTENTS

Margaret as a young girl

Chapter 1

Made-Up Worlds

Margaret liked to
make things up.

Her big brother, Gratz,
liked to play with
things that moved.
He had a toy steamboat
and a big train set.

Her little sister, Roberta,
liked to study and learn.

But Margaret liked to
make up things.

The Brown children
went to bed early.
But Margaret didn't
go to sleep right away.
She made up games
for herself and Roberta
and their cat, Ole King Cole.

Sometimes Margaret read
fairy tales to Roberta.
But she didn't read
what was in the book.
She made up her own
stories from the tales.

Margaret (right) with Roberta and their dog Bruce

In the woods nearby,
Margaret made up plays.
She and Roberta
and Bruce, their pet
collie, acted them out
for other children.

But there were not
many other children around
Beechurst, Long Island.
Margaret didn't have
many school friends either.
She changed schools too often.

So she spent a lot
of time playing alone.

Margaret loved the outdoors.
She loved the trees and
wildflowers in the woods.
She loved the ocean
and she loved animals.

The Brown children had
Ole King Cole and Bruce.
They also had pet rabbits.
Sometimes they had
twenty rabbits at once.

Margaret loved
the trees and
wildflowers
that grew in
the woods where
she played.

Margaret
loved rabbits.

Margaret liked to hold them
and feel their soft fur.

But most of all,
when Margaret was alone,
she liked to make up things.

Much later, she wrote
that when she was a child,
she often lived in
"countries of the worlds
I made up."

Margaret and Roberta went to school in Lausanne, Switzerland.

Chapter 2

Young "Tim"

Margaret's father, Robert,
traveled for his business.
When Margaret was 13, he
took a long trip to India.
Margaret's mother, Maude,
went with him.

So Margaret and Roberta
spent two years at a
girls' school in Switzerland.
Gratz was already at a
boarding school in America.

Margaret didn't like all
the changes in her life.
She wanted things
to stay the same.
But the girls went
to yet another school.

At last, in 1926,
they settled at Dana Hall,
a school in Massachusetts.
Teachers there believed
in teaching girls to
think for themselves.

Margaret liked sports. This gym class
is from Dana Hall, about 1927.

Margaret did pretty well
with her studies.
She did very well at sports.

Margaret liked
her classmates too.
They called her "Tim,"
because her hair was
the color of timothy hay.

MARGARET W. BROWN "Tim"
Great Neck, Long Island, N.Y.

President of Athletic Association, 1927–28; Christian Association; French Club; Captain of Class Hockey Team, 1926; Varsity Hockey Team, 1926, 1927; Assistant Coach of Junior Spread Play, 1927; T. K. D.

When Margaret and Roberta graduated from Dana Hall, their father said they couldn't go to college. He thought girls should just get married.

ROBERTA B. BROWN "Bert"
Great Neck, Long Island, N.Y.

Future—Vassar

Athletic Association; Christian Association; French Club; Class Hockey Team, 1926, 1927; Chairman of Flower Committee, Junior Spread, 1927; Treasurer of T. K. D.

These photographs of Margaret and Roberta came from the 1928 Dana Hall yearbook.

15

The main building of Hollins College

Maude did not agree.
So the girls went to college.
Margaret chose Hollins College
near Roanoke, Virginia.
It was a small school
and she was happy there.

At Hollins, people still
called Margaret "Tim."
They liked her and
the silly things she did.

Margaret didn't always
do well at her studies.
She even failed chemistry.
But her teachers
liked her anyway.

Margaret was
called "Tim"
because her
blond hair was
the color of
timothy hay.

One teacher said Margaret
might become a writer.
That made Margaret feel good.

Margaret planned to
marry a young lawyer
when she finished college.
Then she changed her mind.

Margaret
graduated from
Hollins College
in 1932.

At last, in 1932,
Margaret moved back
to her parents' home
in Great Neck, New York.
She didn't know
what to do next.

Chapter 3

The First Books

For a few years,
Margaret felt mixed up.

First she lived at home,
then in New York City.
She worked in a store.
She studied art.
She tried to write,
but she just couldn't do it.

Opposite page: New York City in 1931

Then, in 1935, she joined
the Bank Street program.
Bank Street was a place
in New York City where
people learned to teach
children in new ways.

Lucy Mitchell started Bank Street.
She thought teachers
should watch how children
act and learn.
They should listen to
how children use words.

Lucy thought
little children
needed stories
about their
everyday world.
So she wrote the
*Here and Now
Story Book*.

Margaret liked Lucy
and her ideas.
Lucy liked Margaret too.
She thought Margaret
could write for children.

Lucy was right.
In 1937, Margaret sold
her first children's book,
When the Wind Blew.
It is about an old lady
and her kitten.

At Bank Street, Margaret
met William Scott.
He became a publisher
and Margaret helped him
find good children's stories.
She wrote some too.

Margaret Wise Brown

She wrote
Bumble Bugs and Elephants
and *The Little Fireman,*
and William published them.

Of course, Margaret
didn't work all the time.
She traveled to Europe.
She lived on an island
off the coast of Maine.
And she went "beagling."

"Beagling" was running
through the woods
as fast as she could
to catch a rabbit.
It was great exercise.
Margaret loved it.

In 1939, Margaret wrote
The Noisy Book
about a dog called Muffin.
It sold very well.
Margaret kept writing.

First he heard the big noises

MEN HAMMERING
Bang bang bang

AUTOMOBILE HORNS
Awuurra awuurra

HORSES HOOFS
Clop clop Clop clop

ANOTHER LITTLE DOG
Bow wow wow

It was a BABY DOLL

And they gave the baby doll
to Muffin for his very own.

STORY
M.W. BROWN
PICTURES
L. WEISGARD

In *The Noisy Book*, a little dog
named Muffin has a bandage on
his eyes. He cannot see, but
he can hear. He hears noises
all around him, including a
funny squeaking sound. What
could that funny sound be? Read
The Noisy Book and find out.

The RUNAWAY BUNNY

by Margaret Wise Brown

Pictures by Clement Hurd

In *The Runaway Bunny*, a little bunny tells his mother what he will be when he runs away. But no matter where he goes or what he does, Mother Bunny says she will find him and be there for him. In the end, the little bunny decides to stay home with his loving parent.

"If you run after me," said the little bunny, "I will become a fish in a trout stream and I will swim away from you."

"If you become a fish in a trout stream," said his mother, "I will become a fisherman and I will fish for you."

The Runaway Bunny
came out in 1942.
It's a wonderful story
about a little rabbit
and his mother.
Margaret *did* like rabbits.

She wrote *A Child's
Good Night Book* on
the back of an envelope.
It was so good that
a publisher bought it right away.

At last Margaret
had found her place
in the world.
Or had she?

Margaret Wise Brown's "Only House" in Maine

Chapter 4

Goodnight Moon

Margaret wasn't always happy.
She had many friends.
But she often felt lonely.
Sometimes she fell in love.
But it never worked out.

Margaret bought herself
a summer house on an island
off the coast of Maine.
She called it the Only House.

In Maine, surrounded by nature's beauty, Margaret got ideas for new stories.

The Only House wasn't fancy.
It had no electricity,
no phone, and no bathroom.
But nature was all around.
That made Margaret happy.

She wrote a book
about this summer home,
The Little Island.

Then Margaret found
an old farm cottage,
right in the middle
of New York City.
It was called Cobble Court.

Margaret rented it
as a place to work.
Upstairs, a friend
of hers made toys.

One morning in 1946,
Margaret woke up
and wrote a story—
just like that!
She called it *Goodnight Moon*.

In the great green room
There was a telephone
And a red balloon
And a picture of—

In *Goodnight Moon,* a little bunny says
goodnight to all the things in his room.

Goodnight room

Goodnight to the kittens and the bears and the mouse.
Goodnight to a comb and a brush and a bowl of mush.

Goodnight clocks
And goodnight s

Margaret didn't know
that almost fifty years later,
children would still beg
to hear about
"the great green room" and
"the old lady whispering 'hush.'"

Goodnight to the old lady whispering "hush."

STORY BY
Margaret Wise Brown
PICTURES BY
Garth Williams

Children also
liked Margaret's
Little Fur Family.
One little boy even tried
to feed his dinner
to the book!

In *Little Fur Family*,
the big fur father
and mother watch over
their little fur child.

And just as the darkness
got very dark
he bumped into his
big fur mother
and she took her little
fur child
home in her arms
and gave him his supper.

THE IMPORTANT BOOK

The important thing
about a daisy is
that it is white.
It is yellow in the middle,
it has long white petals,
and bees sit on it,
it has a ticklish smell,
it grows in green fields,
and there are always
lots of daisies.
But the important thing
about a daisy is
that it is white.

Words by Margaret Wise Brown • Pictures by Leonard Weisgard

Before long, Margaret wrote
Wait Till the Moon Is Full
and *The Important Book.*

Maybe Margaret wasn't
always happy herself.
But she knew how
to make children happy.

Margaret loved the woods and fields.

Chapter 5

A Short Life

Margaret once wrote that
"A good picture book . . .
can almost be whistled."

She began to write songs,
lots of songs.
She also wrote *Mister Dog*,
a funny book about a
"dog who belonged to himself."

Then, in 1952, Margaret
fell in love again.
The man was James Rockefeller.
Margaret called him Pebble.
He loved her too, and
they planned to get married.

But first, Margaret took
a trip to Italy and France.
While she was in France,
she became very ill.
She had to have an operation.

Margaret became ill in Nice, France.

It went well.
Each day, Margaret felt better.
She wrote funny letters
to her friends.

But on the morning
of November 13, 1952,
something went wrong.
Margaret blacked out.
A minute later, she died.

Margaret Wise Brown
was only 42 years old
when she died.
But during her short life,
she wrote more than 100 books
for young children.

THE NOISY B

GOODNIGHT MOON

STORY
M.W. BROWN
PICTURES
L. WEISGARD

by Margaret Wise Brown
Pictures by Clement Hurd
Harper & Row, Publishers

LITTLE FUR FAMILY

Some of those books
will live as long as
there are children around
to ask for them.

The RUNAWAY BUNNY

by Margaret Wise Brown

Pictures by Clement Hurd

THE IMPORTANT BOOK

Words by Margaret Wise Brown

Important Dates

1910   May 23—Born in Brooklyn, New York, to Maude and Robert Brown

1923   Went to school in Lausanne, Switzerland

1926   Entered Dana Hall in Wellesley, Massachusetts

1928   Entered Hollins College, near Roanoke, Virginia

1935   Began work in Bank Street Cooperative School for Student Teachers

1937   *When the Wind Blew* published

1942   *The Runaway Bunny* published

1947   *Goodnight Moon* published

1952   November 13—Died in Nice, France

INDEX

Page numbers in boldface type indicate illustrations.

PHOTO CREDITS

ABOUT THE AUTHOR

Carol Greene has degrees in English literature and musicology. She has worked in international exchange programs, as an editor, and as a teacher of writing. She now lives in Webster Groves, Missouri, and writes full-time. She has published more than 100 books, including those in the Childrens Press Rookie Biographies series.